Counted Cross–Stitch Designs for the Home

ALSO BY THE AUTHOR
Counted Cross-Stitch Designs for All Seasons

Counted Cross-Stitch Designs for the Home

Jana Hauschild Lindberg

CHARLES SCRIBNER'S SONS   NEW YORK

✕ *To My Family*

Copyright © 1985 Jana Hauschild Lindberg

Library of Congress Cataloging in Publication Data

Lindberg, Jana Hauschild.
  Counted cross-stitch designs for the home.

  1. Cross-stitch—Patterns.   I. Title.
TT778.C76L562   1985   746.44   85-8186
ISBN 0-684-18364-1

Published simultaneously in Canada
by Collier Macmillan Canada, Inc.
Copyright under the Berne Convention.

1 3 5 7 9 11 13 15 17 19 H/C 20 18 16 14 12 10 8 6 4 2

Printed in the United States of America.

Contents

THE BEDROOM   63

 # THE BATHROOM   75

THE CHILDREN'S ROOM   85

XXXXXXXXX **Preface**

The purpose of this, my second book published by Scribners, is to present ideas that will embellish and add a personal touch to your home.

In choosing the designs, I have taken into consideration the many complaints I have heard throughout my years as a designer from elderly people who find it difficult to work on fine fabrics. So, while some of the designs require good eyesight (since they have to be sewn on fine fabrics for satisfactory results), others, like some of the ideas for children's rooms, may be done on coarse fabrics—even coarser than those I have suggested—without changing their general appearance. However, always be careful to choose a quality of thread in keeping with the coarseness of your material: the stitches should preferably cover the fabric. I hope, therefore, that nothing will prevent *all* grandparents—because counted cross stitch is not an exclusively feminine pastime—from knowing the joy of creating attractive gifts.

You will find in the designs a large variety of motifs that may be adapted to fit your home and your own ideas. There are easy designs for those who wish to try counted cross stitch for the first time, and more difficult tasks for experienced cross-stitch fans. Some of the designs will require many hours' work, while others can be finished in an evening. Whatever the time you wish to give to it, counted cross stitch is a fascinating pastime that absorbs you completely. It is the best possible therapy—pure relaxation!

 # Introduction

MATERIALS

The designs in this book are created for counted cross stitch, an ancient technique that is very simple to learn and that requires few materials. You will need a fabric that is evenly woven, on which it is easy to count the threads (Figure 1). If you use a fabric that is not evenly woven, your embroidery will be distorted vertically or horizontally (Figures 2 and 3). Most of the designs in this book have been worked on linen that measures 25 threads per inch (10 threads per centimeter). You can select other types of fabric with different thread counts, but you may need to use more strands of embroidery yarn in the needle than are indicated in the instructions to cover the fabric completely. The formula on page 11 shows how to calculate the size of the finished piece if you use a fabric other than the one suggested.

Other supplies you will need are a blunt tapestry needle (#24 or #26); embroidery yarn (the graphs have been keyed to shades of DMC yarn throughout the book; you can substitute another brand by comparing its shades of yarn with the color plate of the design); an embroidery hoop; and a pair of sharp embroidery scissors, which is useful for cutting out mistakes. Some of the projects require brass or bamboo fittings, additional material for backing, and the like—indicated in the instructions for each design.

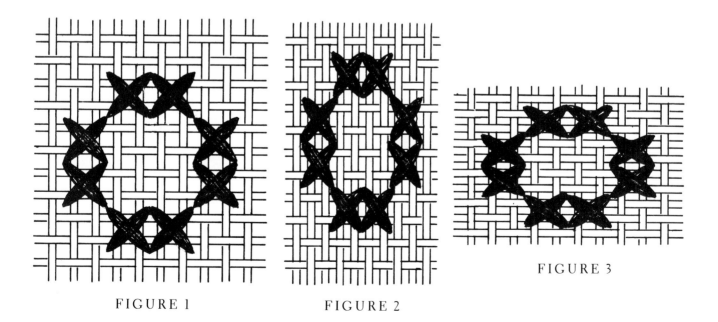

FIGURE 1

FIGURE 2

FIGURE 3

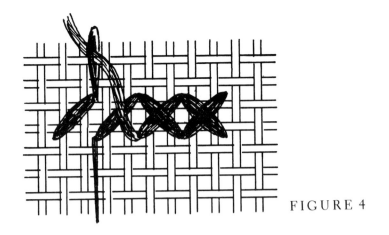

FIGURE 4

FIGURE 5

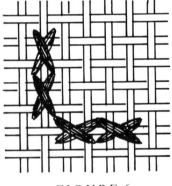

FIGURE 6

TECHNIQUE

Cross stitches are little **X**'s that cover two threads horizontally and two vertically. All understitches are made in one direction and all the overstitches in the opposite direction (Figure 4). The Danish and American style is to begin understitches from left to right, crossing back from right to left; the British style is the reverse. It makes no difference, as long as you are consistent throughout the embroidery.

You can work all the bottom stitches first and then all the top stitches, or you can cross each stitch individually (more yarn will be used if you do the latter). For a vertical row one cross stitch wide, each stitch must be crossed individually (Figure 5).

When starting or ending a piece of yarn, do not tie a knot in it; the knot would show from the right side of the work. Start the first piece of yarn by leaving a tail long enough to thread back into the needle later on, after you have stitched a few rows. Then rethread the needle and weave the tail into the backs of several stitches. Start and fasten off subsequent pieces of yarn by weaving them into the backs of stitches in the same way. Clip the ends close with embroidery scissors, being careful not to cut any of the stitches.

In some places the designs call for half stitches, which are either worked over two threads horizontally and one vertically, or over one thread horizontally and two vertically (Figure 6). Three-quarter cross stitches are illustrated in Figure 7.

Backstitches are sewn over two threads, just as the cross stitches are, in the direction indicated on the graph (Figure 8).

FIGURE 7

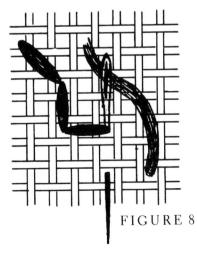

FIGURE 8

WORKING THE DESIGNS

Overcast the raw edges of the linen to prevent fraying. Find the center of the fabric by folding it in half in both directions and creasing it. Find the center of the design by following the arrows on the graph until they intersect. Directions on where to begin stitching each design are given with the project instructions. Be sure the fabric is oriented to match the design; you don't want to discover too late that you are stitching a vertical design on a horizontal piece of material.

Embroidery should proceed toward the sides and downward, never upward. To embroider the top half of a design that you have started in the middle, turn the work and the graph 180° (upside down); don't forget to turn the graph symbols as well. The slant of the stitches will then be the same throughout the embroidery. If you prefer to work downward from the top of the design, count up from the center. Every square on the graph is a full cross stitch on the fabric, so count two threads for each square.

To stitch the embroidery on a fabric other than the 25-count linen recommended in the instructions, calculate how large the finished piece will be according to this formula:

Multiply the piece's finished measurement (given in the instructions) by the number of threads per inch in the linen it is sewn on. Then divide that figure by the number of threads per inch in the fabric you want to sew on.

Thus, if a piece is 6 × 6″ on 25-count linen and you want to stitch it on a fabric with 18 threads to the inch, calculate as follows: 6 × 25 = 150 ÷ 18 = 8.3. The finished piece will be approximately 8¼ inches square. Remember when you are cutting fabric to allow a generous margin, 2 inches or so all around.

FINISHING

When the embroidery is finished, wash it in lukewarm water with mild soap. Rinse it well, adding a little vinegar to the last rinse. Do not wring. Roll the embroidery up in a towel and gently press out the excess water. Spread the piece right side down on your ironing board, cover it with a thin, slightly moistened cloth, and iron until both cloth and embroidery are dry.

Instructions for hemming the embroideries and for other finishing touches are given with each project.

The Living Room

✕✕ FLORAL BELL PULL

See Plate 1.

Finished size: 5½ × 35″ (14 × 88 cm.)
Cutting size: 8 × 40″ (20 × 100 cm.)
Cutting size (interfacing): 5½ × 7″ (14 × 18 cm.)

Materials

Linen with 25 threads/in. (10/cm.)
DMC embroidery yarn, 1 skein of each color, except 2 skeins of 471 light
   green
Brass finishings (can be bought at any needlecraft or crafts supply store)

Instructions

Fold the fabric in half lengthwise to find the middle. Measure 2 inches (5 cm.) from the top of the fabric and begin embroidering at the arrow on the graph. Use two strands of yarn in the needle. Repeat the motif using Plate 1 as a model. Press the finished embroidery. Place the interfacing on the wrong side of the work and fold the linen over 5 threads from the border. Sew it down with small stitches. Make casings at the top and bottom for the bell-pull fitting.

DMC yarn

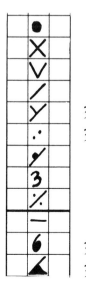

●	937	dark green
✕	470	medium green
V	471	light green
╱	472	lightest green
Y	3052	medium blue-green
∴	3053	light blue-green
✔	792	dark blue
3	798	medium blue
⁒	799	light blue
—	809	lightest blue
6	3685	darkest rose
◣	3350	dark clear rose

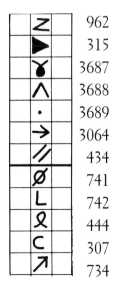

Z	962	medium clear rose
▶	315	dark red-brown
Y	3687	dark rose
∧	3688	medium rose
•	3689	light rose
→	3064	light brown
∥	434	medium brown
Ø	741	orange
L	742	light orange
♀	444	clear yellow
C	307	light bright yellow
↗	734	light olive

REPEAT

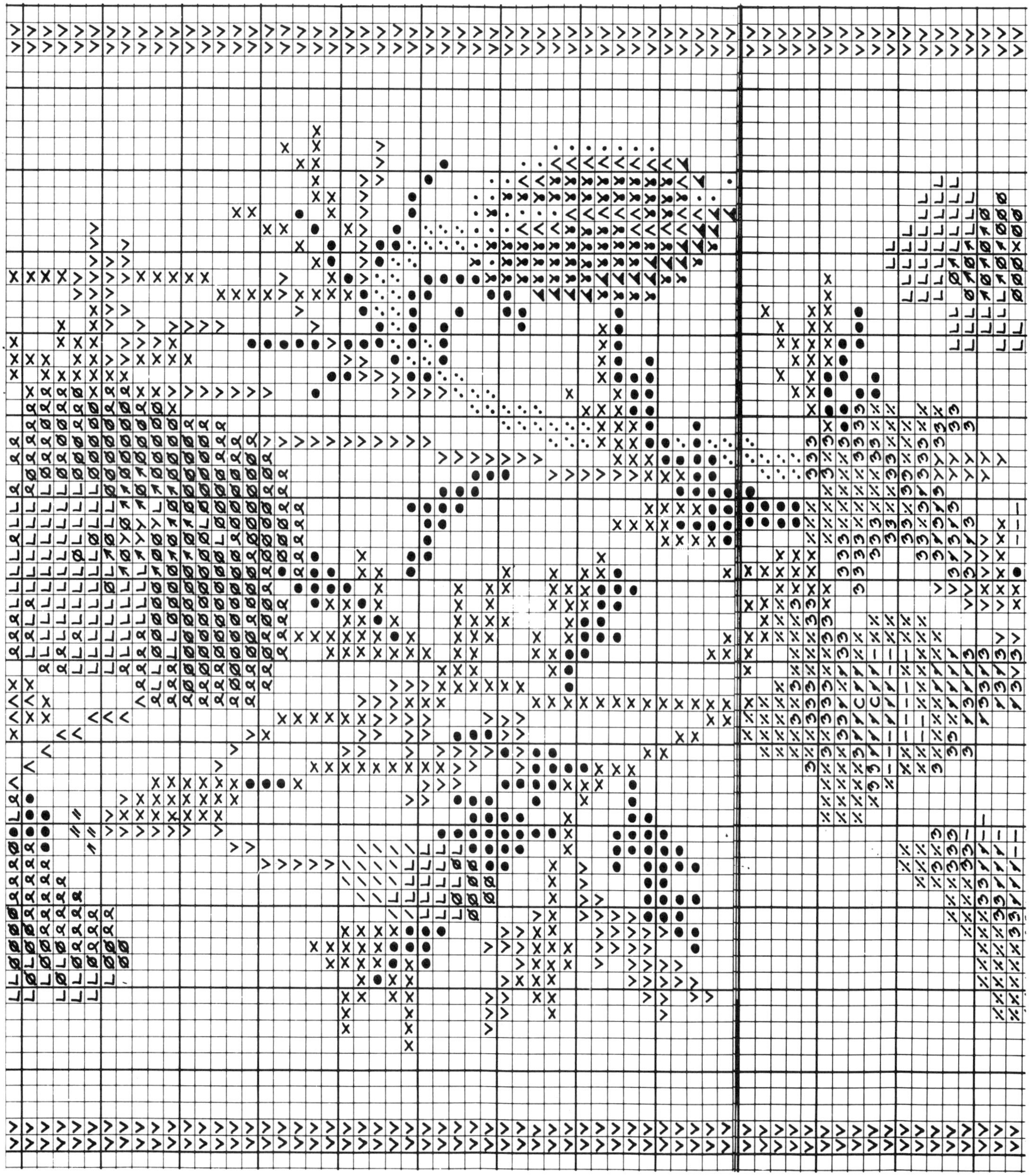

FLORAL BELL PULL
(BOTTOM HALF)

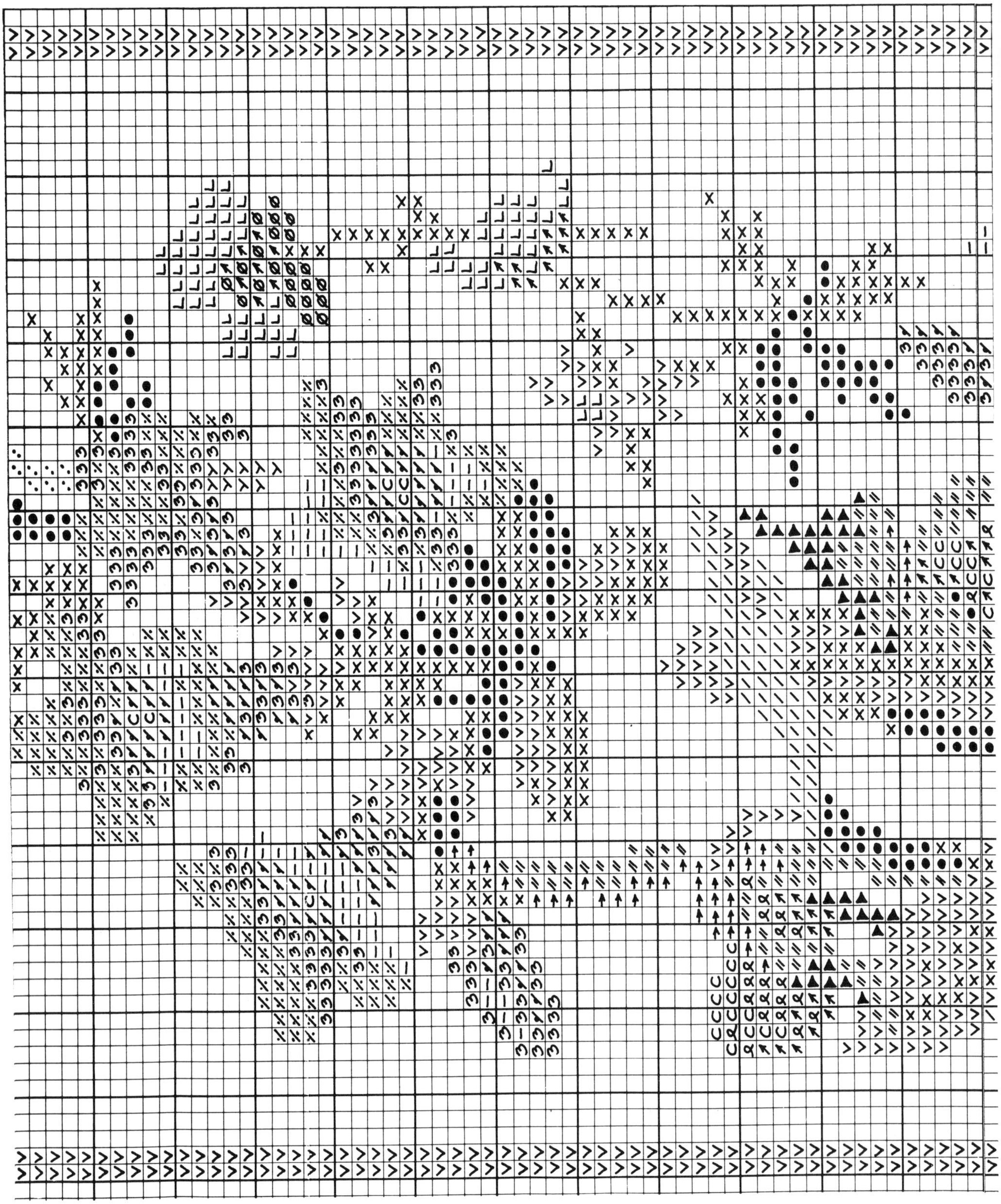

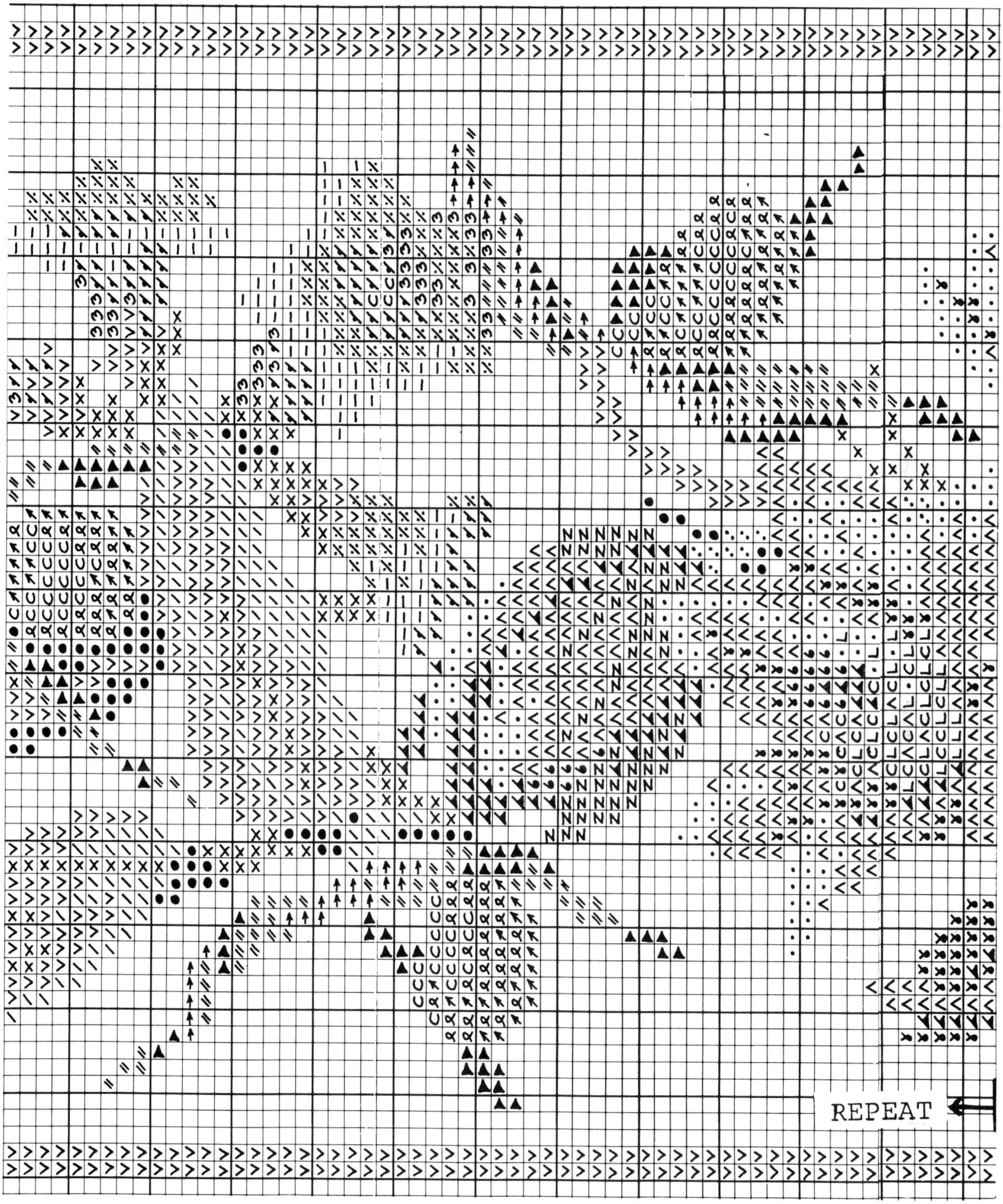
REPEAT

✕✕ TULIP CHAIR COVER

See Plate 2.

Finished size and cutting size depend on the size of your chair. See the formula on page 11 to estimate size.

Materials

Linen with 25 threads/in. (10/cm.)
DMC embroidery yarn, 2 skeins of each color except 3 skeins of DMC 3347
Medium green and DMC 471 light green
Chair with a removable seat

Instructions

Place a sheet of paper over your chair seat and draw the outline. Leave 4 inches (10 cm.) extra on all sides for the turned-in edge and ¼ inch (1 cm.) casing. Place the pattern on your linen and baste on the outline. Find the center of the fabric and the center of one tulip and begin from there. Use 2 strands of yarn in the needle over 2 threads of fabric. Iron the finished embroidery. Thread a rubber band or string through the casing, recover the seat, and pull the string to make the cover tight. Fasten the seat onto the chair.

DMC yarn

Symbol	DMC	Color
◥	3346	dark green
∥	3347	medium green
✕	471	light green
∣	3348	lightest green
●	3688	red lilac
+	778	light lilac
▬	761	dark rose
∧	754	medium rose
╱	948	light rose
K	676	golden
O	727	yellow
∴	3078	light yellow

TULIP CHAIR COVER

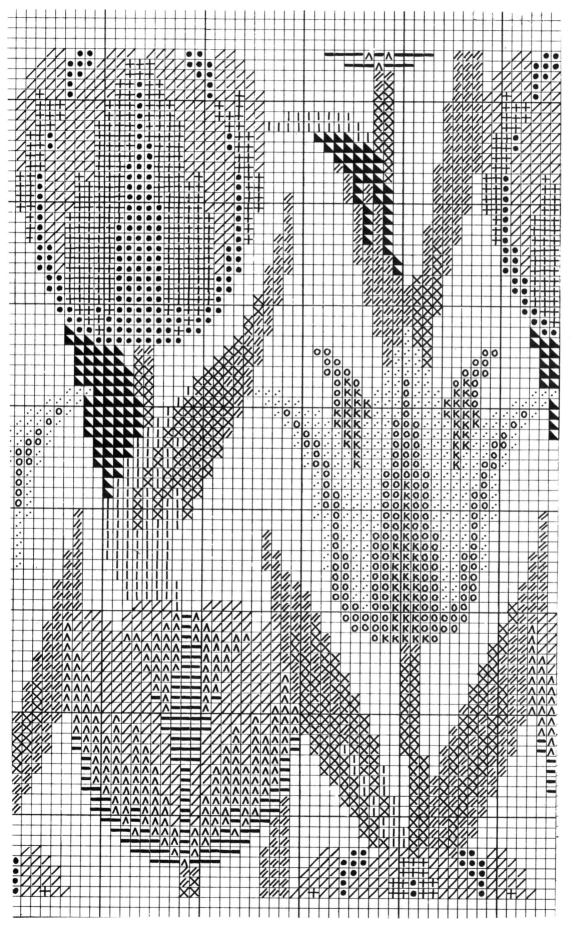

✕✕ TABLE RUNNER WITH LEAVES

See Plate 3.

Finished size: 6³/₄ × 20″ (17 × 50 cm.)
Cutting size: 9 × 22″ (22 × 55 cm.)

Materials

Linen with 20 threads/in. (8/cm.)
DMC embroidery yarn, pearl #5 and gold metal thread, 4 skeins. Use 368
    for cross stitches and the gold thread for backstitches
    Cross stitches are sewn with 1 thread pearl yarn or 3 threads embroi-
    dery floss (the floss is also 368).

Instructions

Fold the fabric in half lengthwise to find the middle. Measure 1⁵/₈ inches (4 cm.) from the top of the fabric and begin embroidering using the graph as a guide. Leave 1⁵/₈ inches (4 cm.) at each end for a fringe. Make a narrow hem on the long sides. Iron the finished embroidery.

DMC yarn

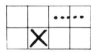

         gold thread
368   pearl yarn #5, light green

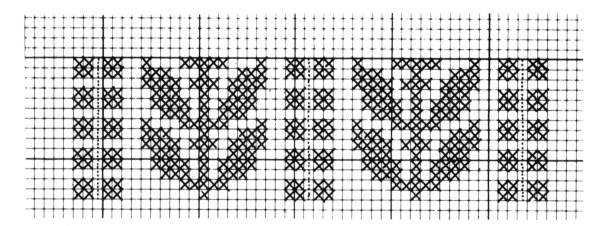

✕✕ WALLHANGING WITH LINNEA

See Plate 4.

Finished size: 9 × 12¼″ (23 × 30.5 cm.)
Cutting size: 11 × 14″ (28 × 35 cm.)

Materials

Linen with 25 threads/in. (10/cm.)
DMC embroidery yarn, 1 skein of each color

Instructions

Find the center of the fabric and of the design and begin embroidering, using 2 strands of yarn in the needle. Iron the finished design and hem the hanging by folding over 5 and then 8 threads to the wrong side. Sew the hem down with small stitches. Glue the embroidery to a light cardboard and fix 2 rings on the back, and one on each corner at the top. Run a string or picture wire through the rings to hang your wallhanging.

DMC yarn

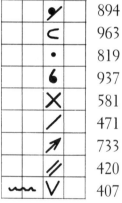

	894	dark rose
	963	medium rose
	819	light rose
	937	dark green
	581	medium green
	471	light green
	733	olive
	420	brown
	407	red-brown

WALLHANGING WITH LINNEA

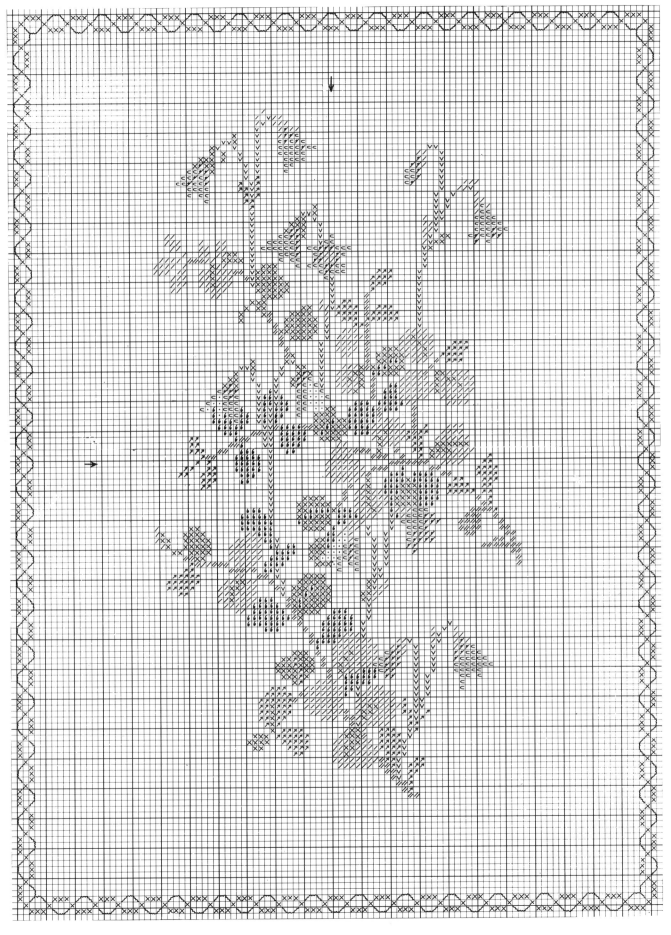

WALLHANGING WITH CHICORY

See Plate 5.

Finished size: 9 × 12¼″ (23 × 30.5 cm.)
Cutting size: 11 × 14″ (28 × 35 cm.)

Materials

Linen with 25 threads/in. (10 threads/cm.)
DMC embroidery yarn, 1 skein of each color

Instructions

Find the center of the fabric and of the design and begin embroidering. Use 2 strands of yarn in the needle. Iron the finished hanging and hem it by folding over 5, then 8 threads to the wrong side and sewing with small stitches. Mount as for the previous project.

DMC yarn

Symbol	DMC	Color
●	930	darkest blue
∠	825	dark blue
∥	518	medium blue
⊂	813	light blue
ↆ	367	dark green
Y	988	medium green
/	3347	light green
•	3348	lightest green
V	223	dull rose

WALLHANGING WITH CHICORY

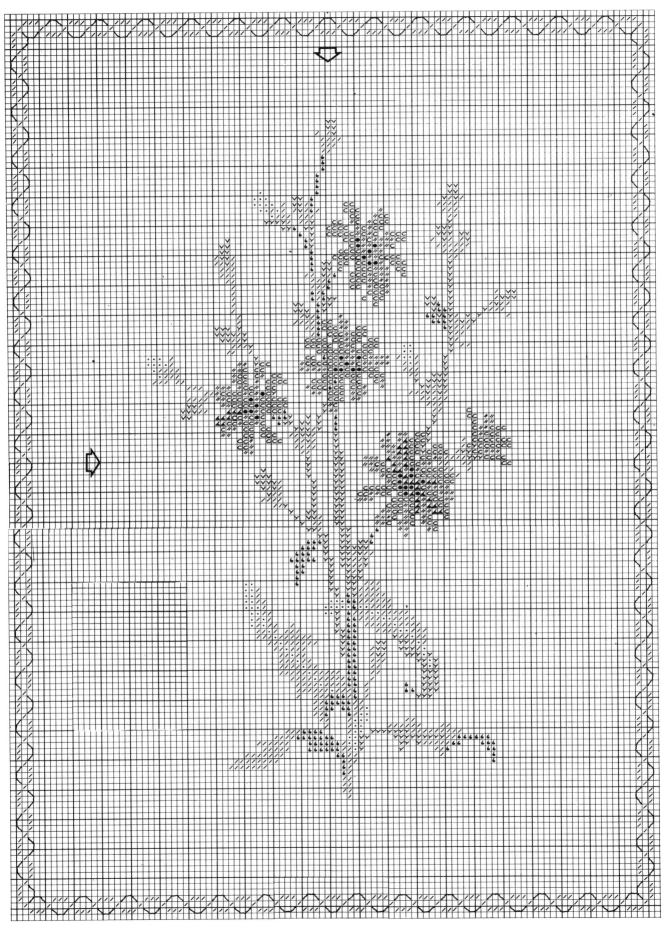

✕✕ CLOTH WITH HAREBELL AND BUTTERFLIES

See Plate 6.

Finished size: 11 × 11″ (28 × 28 cm.)
Cutting size: 13 × 13″ (33 × 33 cm.)

Materials

Beige linen with 25 threads/in. (10/cm.)
DMC embroidery yarn, 1 skein of each color

Instructions

Find the center of the material and of the design and begin embroidering, using 2 strands of yarn in the needle. Iron the finished cloth and hem by folding over 5 and 8 threads to the wrong side and sewing with small stitches.

DMC yarn

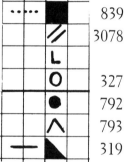

•••••	839	dark brown
⁄⁄	3078	yellow
L		white
O	327	red lilac
●	792	blue
∧	793	light blue
▬	319	dark green

CLOTH WITH HAREBELL AND BUTTERFLIES

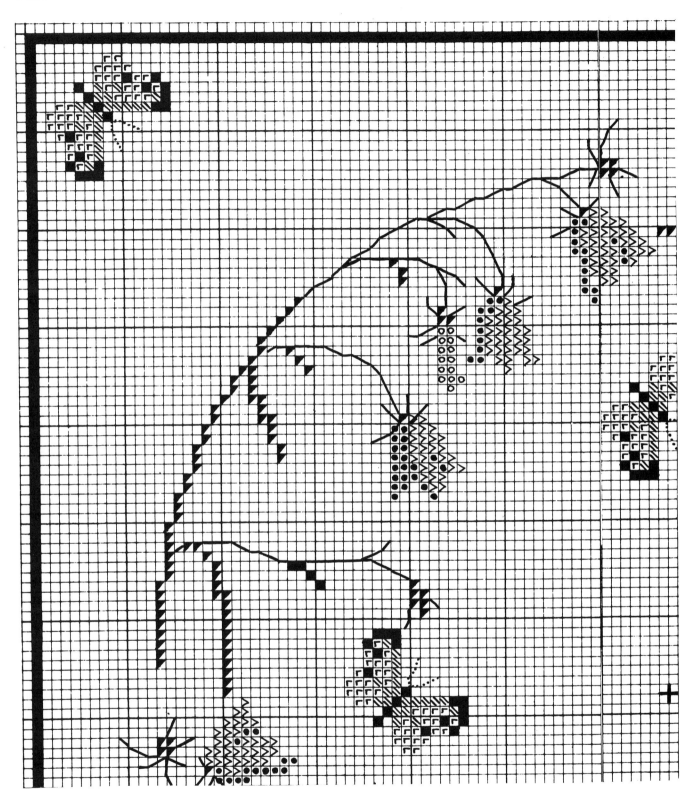

28

✕✕ TABLECLOTH WITH WILD ROSES

See Plate 7.

Finished size: 56 × 56″ (140 × 140 cm.)
Cutting size: 56 × 56″ (140 × 140 cm.)
Wreath size: 22″ (55 cm.)

Materials

Linen with 25 threads/in. (10/cm.)
DMC embroidery yarn (number of skeins given below)

Instructions

Find the center of the fabric and of the design; the graphs show one-quarter of the design. Count out to the embroidery from the center. Sew with 2 strands of yarn in the needle over 2 threads of fabric. Iron the finished embroidery. To hem, measure 1½ inches (3 cm.) from the edges and sew one row cross stitches with rose 604, leave a 2-thread space and sew another with green 906. Two threads from the outermost row, stitch around the tablecloth with a sewing machine. Thread the fabric to make a fringe (see graph).

DMC yarn

↙	602	darkest rose, 2 skeins
⟋	603	dark rose, 3 skeins
⌀	604	medium rose, 4 skeins
⊂	894	light rose, 2 skeins
—	776	lightest rose, 2 skeins
Z	950	beige, 1 skein
•	948	light beige, 2 skeins
ℓ	781	golden, 1 skein
╱	742	light orange, 1 skein
3	444	yellow, 1 skein
⅄	733	olive, 1 skein
│	734	light olive, 1 skein
●	986	dark green, 2 skeins
✕	905	medium green, 3 skeins
∨	906	light green, 4 skeins
•ᐧ	907	lightest green, 2 skeins
→	833	light golden, 1 skein

TABLECLOTH WITH
WILD ROSES

machine stitching

fringe

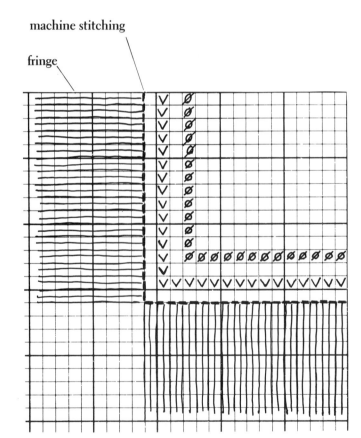

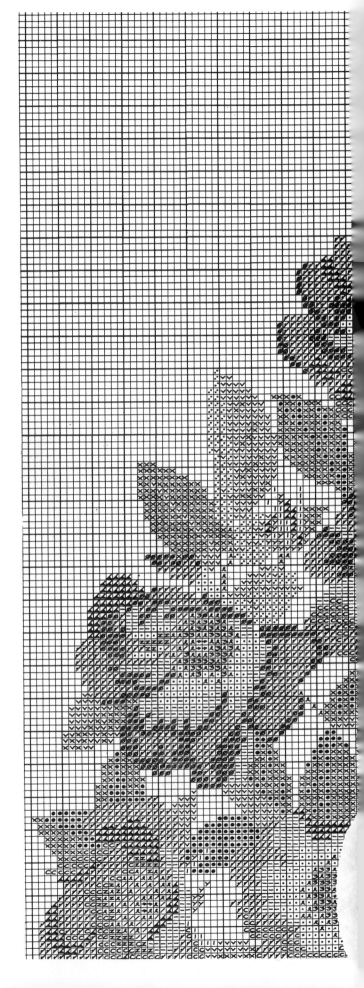

Plate 1. Floral Bell Pull

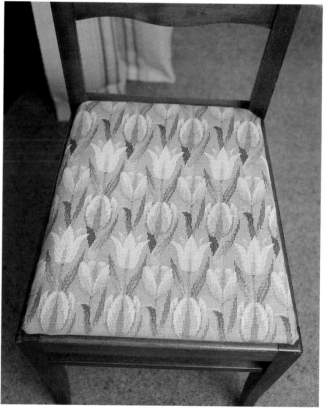

Plate 2. Tulip Chair Cover

Plate 3. Table Runner with Leaves

Plate 4. Wallhanging with Linnea

Plate 5. Wallhanging with Chicory

Plate 6. Cloth with
Harebell and Butterflies

Plate 7. Tablecloth
with Wild Roses

Plate 8. Tablecloth
in Three Shades of Blue

Plate 9. Poppy Placemat
and Plate Liner

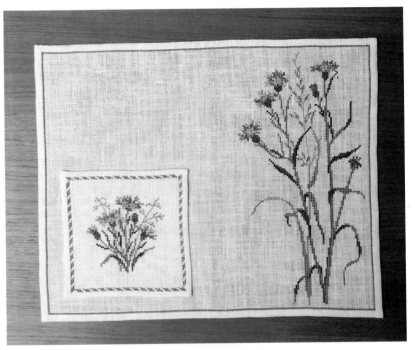

Plate 10. Placemat and
Plate Liner with Cornflowers

Plate 11. Flower Wreath
Napkin Holders

Plate 12.
Romanian Tablecloth

Plate 13. Tray Cloth
with Violets

Plate 14. Tea Cosy, Placemat, and Napkin with Nightingales

Plate 15. Square Potholder with Daisy

Plate 16. Round Potholder with Blue Flowers

Plate 17.
Kitchen Mitt with Rooster

Plate 18. Chicken Family Shelf Border

Plate 19. Curtain
with Pansy and
Forget-Me-Not

Plate 20. Bulletin Board with Mushrooms

✕✕ TABLECLOTH IN THREE SHADES OF BLUE

See Plate 8.

Finished size: 56 × 56″ (140 × 140 cm.)
Cutting size: 56 × 56″ (140 × 140 cm.)

Materials

Linen with 20 threads/in. (8/cm.)
DMC embroidery yarn, 6 skeins of each color

Instructions

Find the center of your material and follow the arrows to find the center of the design. Begin embroidering from there using 3 strands of yarn in the needle. There should be 16 rosettes centered on the tablecloth. Embroider the border 2 inches (5 cm.) from the edge of the fabric, fraying 1 inch later for fringe.

You can also make this tablecloth in shades of green (DMC 701, 703, 704) or orange (DMC 900, 947, 740).

DMC yarn

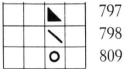

797   dark blue
798   medium blue
809   light blue

TABLECLOTH IN THREE SHADES OF BLUE

✕✕ POPPY PLACEMAT

See Plate 9.

Finished size: 13 × 16½″ (33 × 41 cm.)
Cutting size: 16 × 20″ (40 × 50 cm.)

Materials

Linen with 25 threads/in. (10/cm.)
DMC embroidery yarn, one skein of each color

Instructions

Begin embroidering the border 25 threads from the top and the side of the fabric using 2 strands of yarn in the needle. Finish the design according to the graph. Iron the finished embroidery and hem the placemat. From the outside of the border count 21 threads and cut away the surplus fabric. Fold over 4 and then 7 threads to the wrong side of the work and sew with small stitches.

DMC yarn

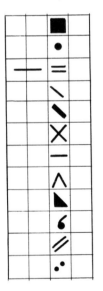

830	brown
831	dark golden
833	medium golden
834	light golden
3346	dark green
3347	medium green
3053	gray-green
733	olive
349	darkest red
350	dark red
351	medium red
352	light red

✕✕ POPPY PLATE LINER

See Plate 9.

Finished size: 6 × 6″ (15 × 15 cm.)
Cutting size: 8 × 8″ (20 × 20 cm.)

Materials

Linen with 25 threads/in. (10/cm.)
DMC embroidery yarn, one skein of each color

Instructions

Find the center of the fabric and of the design and begin embroidering, using 2 strands of yarn in the needle over 2 threads of fabric. Press the finished embroidery. From the outside of the border count 21 threads and cut away the surplus fabric. Fold over 4 and then 7 threads to the wrong side of the work and sew with small stitches.

DMC yarn

❏	987	dark green
✕	320	medium green
—	471	light green
o	734	golden
■	310	black
`	350	red
L	351	light red
— //	3012	olive

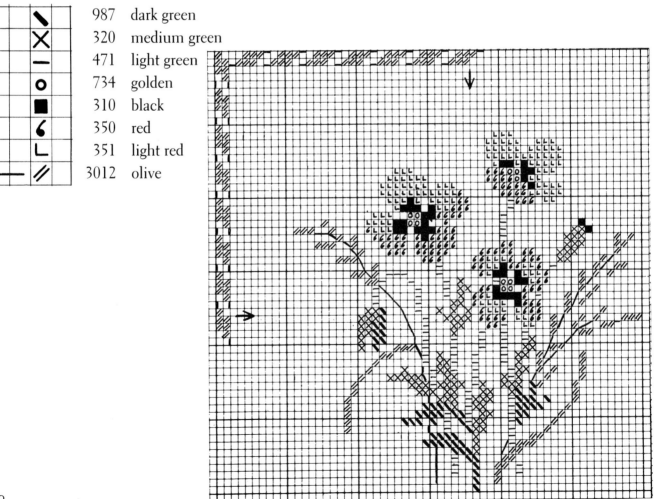

✕✕ PLACEMAT WITH CORNFLOWERS

See Plate 10.

Finished size: 13 × 16½″ (33 × 41 cm.)
Cutting size: 16 × 20″ (40 × 50 cm.)

Materials

Linen with 25 threads/in. (10/cm.)
DMC embroidery yarn, one skein of each color

Instructions

Find the center of the fabric and of the design and begin embroidering, using 2 strands of yarn in the needle over 2 threads of fabric. Press the finished embroidery. From the outside of the border count 21 threads and cut away surplus fabric. Fold over 4 and then 7 threads to the wrong side of the work and sew with small stitches.

DMC yarn

	830	dark golden
Ø	831	medium golden
⫶	833	light golden
3	733	medium olive
V	734	light olive
6	501	dark green
//	367	medium green
C	3347	light green
—	3052	light gray-green
◢	792	dark blue
I	793	medium blue
∴	794	light blue
⚭	917	red lilac

PLACEMAT WITH CORNFLOWERS

✕✕ PLATE LINER WITH CORNFLOWERS

See Plate 10.

Finished size: 6 × 6" (15 × 15 cm.)
Cutting size: 8 × 8" (20 × 20 cm.)

Materials

Linen with 25 threads/in. (10/cm.)
DMC embroidery yarn, one skein of each color

Instructions

Find the center of the fabric and of the design and begin embroidering, using 2 strands of yarn in the needle over 2 threads of fabric. Press the finished embroidery. From the outside of the border count 21 threads and cut away surplus fabric. Fold over 4 and then 7 threads to the wrong side of the work and sew with small stitches.

DMC yarn

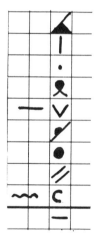

792	dark blue
793	medium blue
809	light blue
917	red lilac
316	faded rose
830	dark golden
3345	dark green
367	medium green
3347	light green
3052	light gray-green

×× FLOWER WREATH NAPKIN HOLDERS

See Plate 11.

Cutting size: 4 × 6½″ (10 × 16 cm.)

Materials

Linen, 25 threads/in. (10/cm.)
DMC embroidery floss, one skein of each color
Lace, 16 inches (40 cm.)

Instructions

Find the center of the fabric and of the design and embroider from there. Use 2 strands of floss in the needle. Iron the finished embroidery. Place the ends of the piece together, right sides facing, and stitch them together. Fold the linen to the wrong side, 4 threads from either side of the motif. Hem the lace onto either side of the napkin ring.

DMC *yarn*

906   green
335   red (or 798 blue)
444   yellow

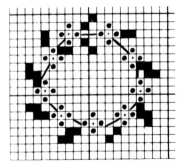

✕✕ ROMANIAN TABLECLOTH

See Plate 12.

Finished size: 52 × 80″ (130 × 200 cm.)
Cutting size: 56 × 84″ (140 × 210 cm.)

Materials

Linen with 25 threads/in. (10/cm.)
DMC embroidery yarn (number of skeins given below)

Instructions

Find the center of the material at one end of the cloth and center your design there. Use 2 strands of yarn in the needle over 2 threads of fabric. Iron the finished tablecloth and hem the edges by folding 1 cm. and then 2 cm. to the wrong side. Stitch using a hemming stitch over 2 threads all around.

DMC yarn

◢	311	dark blue, 6 skeins
/	597	light blue, 7 skeins
۵	347	dark red, 6 skeins
C	223	light red, 6 skeins
V	783	golden, 2 skeins
//	208	lilac, 2 skeins

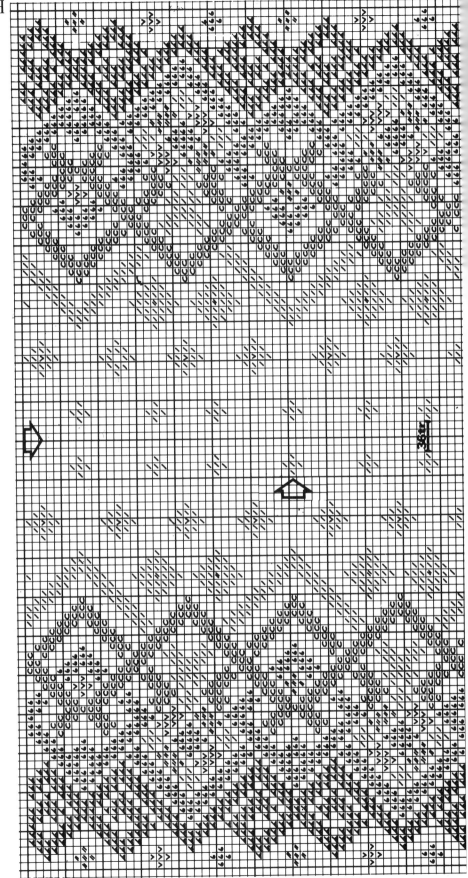

 # TRAY CLOTH WITH VIOLETS

See Plate 13.

Finished size: 15 × 11″ (38 × 27 cm.)
Cutting size: 17 × 12³/₄″ (43 × 32 cm.)

Materials

Linen with 25 threads/in. (10/cm.)
DMC embroidery yarn, one skein of each color

Instructions

Begin embroidering the border 1 inch (2.5 cm.) in from the edge of the fabric, as with the placemats. Use 2 strands of yarn in the needle over 2 threads of fabric. Iron and hem as for placemats.

DMC yarn

◥	3345	darkest green
╱	3346	dark green
✕	3347	medium green
−	471	light green
■	552	dark lilac
●	553	medium lilac
L	554	light lilac
∴	741	orange

TRAY CLOTH WITH VIOLETS

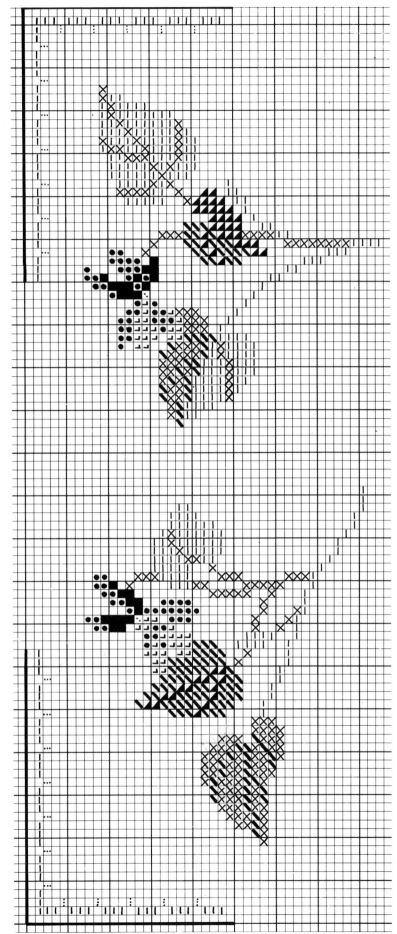

46

The Kitchen

✕✕ TEA COSY WITH NIGHTINGALES

See Plate 14.

Finished size: 12 × 13″ (32 × 27 cm.)
Cutting size (cut two pieces): 14 × 15″ (35 × 38 cm.)
Cutting size for rubber foam (cut two pieces): 12¾ × 11″ (32 × 27 cm.)

Materials

Linen with 25 threads/in. (10/cm.)
DMC embroidery yarn, 1 skein of black, 2 of dark beige, 1 of gray-green,
    1 of green, 1 of dark rose, 1 of light rose, 1 of yellow
Rubber foam, ⅕ inch (1 cm.) thick

Instructions

The measurements given correspond to the tea cosy in Plate 14. You can make your own tea cosy (for your own teapot) in any size, using a symmetrical paper pattern.

Place the pattern on the linen and draw the outline. Count 2 inches (5 cm.) extra on the bottom for the fold-over allowance. Start embroidering from the top with the border in the center. Use 2 strands of yarn in the needle over 2 threads of fabric. Make sure that the motif is symmetrical.

Using the same paper pattern, cut 2 pieces of rubber foam and stitch them together (leaving the bottom open) to form a hood.

Iron the embroidery. Place the 2 pieces of linen right sides together and stitch them together (leaving the bottom open). Turn the "hood" right side out and place over the foam. Fold the extra linen on the bottom over the foam and baste it to the outside.

DMC yarn

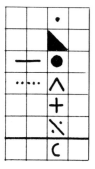

310	black
610	dark beige
3012	gray-green
470	green
899	dark rose
776	light rose
725	yellow

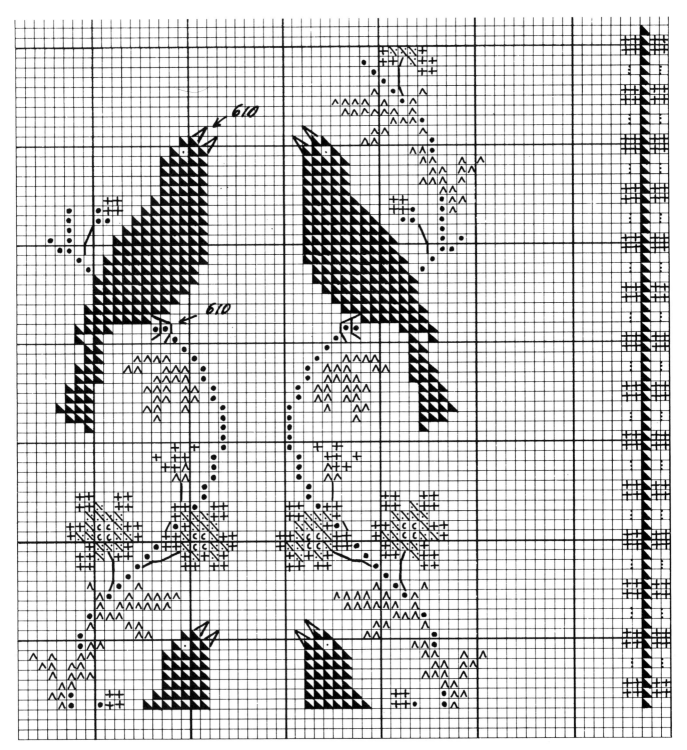

✕✕ PLACEMAT AND NAPKIN WITH NIGHTINGALES

See Plate 14.

PLACEMAT

Finished size: 14 × 18″ (35 × 45 cm.)
Cutting size: 16 × 20″ (40 × 50 cm.)

NAPKIN

Finished size: 10 × 10″ (25 × 25 cm.)
Cutting size: 12 × 12″ (30 × 30 cm.)

Materials

Linen with 25 threads/in. (10/cm.)
DMC embroidery yarn, 1 skein of black, 2 of dark beige, 1 of gray-green,
    1 of green, 1 of dark rose, 1 of light rose, 1 of yellow

Instructions

FOR THE PLACEMAT: Begin embroidering the border about 1 inch (2.5 cm.) from the
edge. Use 2 strands of thread in the needle over 2 threads of fabric. Embroider the nightingales according to the graph. Press the finished embroidery and hem under all the edges.
FOR THE NAPKIN: Begin as with the placemat, and embroider the pink flower in the corner, according to the graph. Iron the finished napkin and hem all the edges.

DMC *yarn*

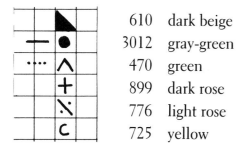

610	dark beige
3012	gray-green
470	green
899	dark rose
776	light rose
725	yellow

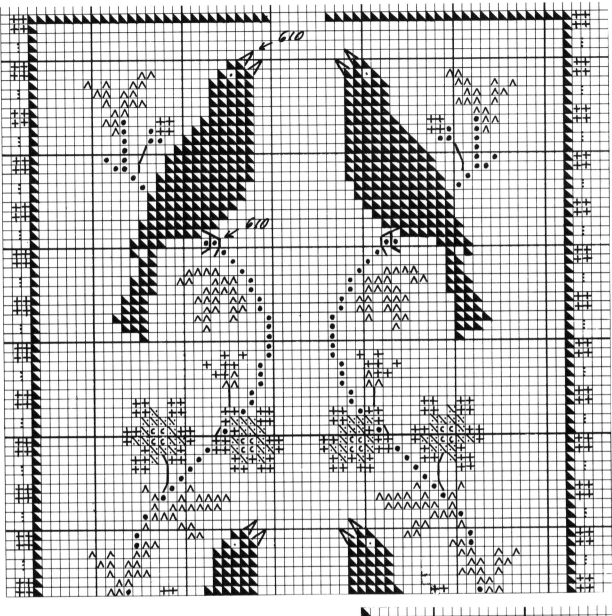

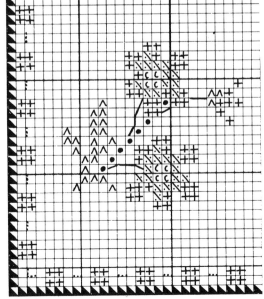

SQUARE POTHOLDER WITH DAISY

See Plate 15.

Finished size: 6¹/₂ × 6¹/₂″ (16 × 16 cm.)
Cutting size (cut two pieces): 8 × 8″ (20 × 20 cm.)

Materials

Linen with 25 threads/in. (10/cm.)
DMC embroidery yarn, one skein of each color
Terry-cloth or insulated material for filling
Colored piping for edges

Instructions

Find the center of your material and of the design and begin embroidering. Iron the finished piece. Baste the front and back sections together (wrong sides facing), with the insulating material in between. Then sew them all together on a machine. Trim away the surplus linen ¹/₈ inch (.3 cm.) from the seam and sew the seam binding on with small stitches on both sides. Leave a 4-inch (10 cm.) loop to hang the potholder with.

DMC yarn

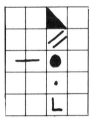

3346	dark green
470	light green
894	dark rose
818	light rose
725	yellow

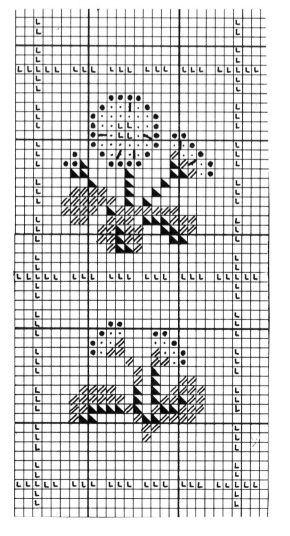

✕✕ ROUND POTHOLDER WITH BLUE FLOWERS

See Plate 16.

Finished size: 6½ inches (16 cm.) in diameter
Cutting size (cut two pieces): 8 × 8″ (20 × 20 cm.)

Materials

Linen with 25 threads/in. (10/cm.)
Terry-cloth or insulated foam material for filling
DMC embroidery yarn, 1 skein of each color
Colored seam binding

Instructions

Stitch the motif in the center of your fabric. Use two strands of thread in the needle over two threads of fabric. Iron the finished embroidery. Draw a circle 16 cm. in diameter around the motif. Sew the front and back sections together, placing the terry-cloth or rubber foam in between. Cut the surplus linen ⅛ inch (.3 cm.) from the outline and sew the seam binding over the seam, stitching it on with small stitches on both sides. Leave 4 inches (10 cm.) for the loop.

DMC yarn

◣	905	dark green
//	906	light green
●	798	dark blue
✕	334	medium blue
│	794	light blue
○	725	yellow

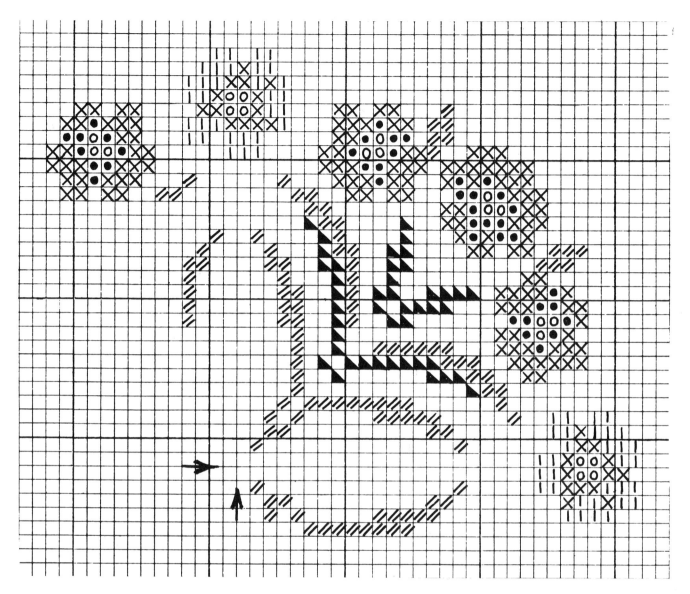

KITCHEN MITT WITH ROOSTER

See Plate 17.

Finished size: 12 × 8″ (30 × 20 cm.)
Cutting size (cut two pieces): 12³/₄ × 9″ (32 × 22.5 cm.)

Materials

Linen with 20 threads/in. (8/cm.)
DMC embroidery yarn, 1 skein of each color. Use three strands in the
  needle.
Terry-cloth or foam insulation
Colored seam binding for finishing, 1 inch (2.5 cm.) broad

Instructions

INSIDE OF GLOVE: Cut 2 layers of interfacing and 2 layers of terry-cloth using the diagram
as a pattern. Zig-zag stitch them together, keeping the terry-cloth outermost.
OUTSIDE OF GLOVE: Trace your pattern on the linen, and begin embroidering at a point
1¹/₂ inches (3 cm.) from the bottom. Press the finished embroidery.

  Stitch the front and back together, right sides facing. Cut the surplus linen ¹/₄ inch
(1 cm.) from the outline, and insert the terry-cloth lining. Baste the seam binding over the
sandwich of materials and zig-zag stitch them all together.

DMC yarn

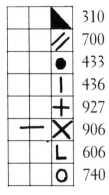

310	black
700	blue-green
433	brown
436	light brown
927	gray
906	yellow-green
606	red
740	orange

KITCHEN MITT WITH ROOSTER

✕✕ CHICKEN FAMILY SHELF BORDER

See Plate 18.

Finished size: 2¹/₂″ (6 cm.) deep and as long as your shelf
Cutting size: 3¹/₈″ (8 cm.) deep

Materials

Linen with 25 threads/in. (10/cm.)
DMC embroidery yarn, one skein of each color
One piece of medium-weight interfacing, such as Pellon® nonwoven
    bonded textiles, the same size as the finished embroidery

Instructions

Stitch the design according to the graph, using 2 strands of yarn in the needle over 2 threads
of fabric. Iron the finished embroidery. Center the interfacing on the wrong side, turn the
edges of the linen to the back, and sew together with small stitches. Glue the border to the
edge of your kitchen shelf.

DMC yarn

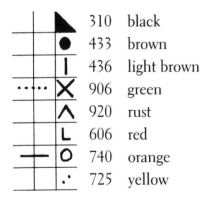

◣	310	black
●	433	brown
❘	436	light brown
✕	906	green
∧	920	rust
L	606	red
O	740	orange
∴	725	yellow

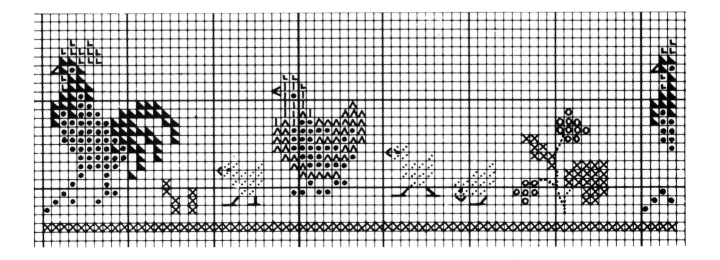

✕✕ CURTAIN WITH PANSY AND FORGET-ME-NOT

See Plate 19.

Finished size: 16″ (40 cm.) and as long as you need
Cutting size: 18″ (45 cm.) deep

Materials

Linen with 20 threads/in. (8/cm.)
DMC embroidery yarn, 2 skeins of very dark lilac, 2 of dark lilac, 2 of medium lilac, 1 of light lilac, 1 of black, 1 of white, 1 of yellow, 2 of blue, 1 of light blue, 1 of dark green, 2 of medium green, 2 of light green, 1 of lightest green. This will cover 3.3 feet (1 meter) of curtain.
Curtain rings, per length (see Instructions)

Instructions

Find the center of the linen on the long side. The center corresponds to the arrow on the diagram. Count 1⅝ inches (4 cm.) from the bottom edge for the hem and begin embroidering the blue line, extending the diagram. Use three strands of yarn in the needle over 2 threads of fabric. The hem on the sides is ⅛ inch (.3 cm.) wide. Sew the curtain rings on the top at about 4½-inch (11 cm.) intervals.

DMC yarn

●	550	darkest lilac
∕∕	552	dark lilac
∧	553	medium lilac
L	210	light lilac
■	310	black
∴		white
○	725	yellow
◢	793	blue
+	794	light blue
◣	580	dark green
‖	581	medium green
⊠	471	light green
—	3348	lightest green

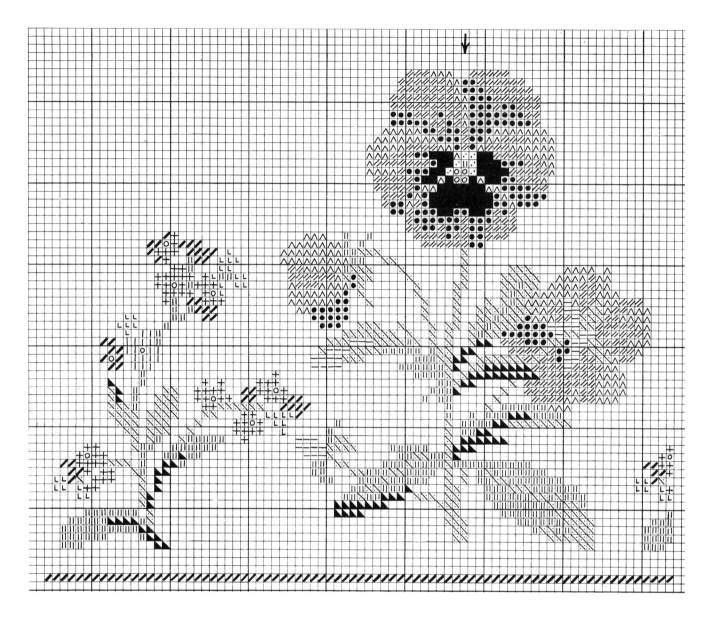

✕✕ BULLETIN BOARD WITH MUSHROOMS

See Plate 20.

Finished size: 24 × 16″ (60 × 40 cm.)
Cutting size: 28 × 20″ (70 × 50 cm.)

Materials

Java cotton about 10 threads/in. (4/cm.)
DMC embroidery yarn, one skein of each color except 2 skeins of DMC
    732 light green
Styrofoam or corkboard, 24 × 16″ (60 × 40 cm.)

Instructions

Begin embroidering the mushroom in the left-hand corner about 3 inches (7 cm.) in from either edge. Use three strands of yarn in the needle. Iron the finished embroidery and center the board on the wrong side. Fold over the excess material and fasten to the back with glue or staples.

DMC yarn

Symbol	No.	Color
— ■	830	dark faded green
✕	732	light faded green
●	606	red
～ +	608	light red
╲	841	dark beige
L	842	light beige
∴	712	ecru

BULLETIN BOARD WITH MUSHROOMS

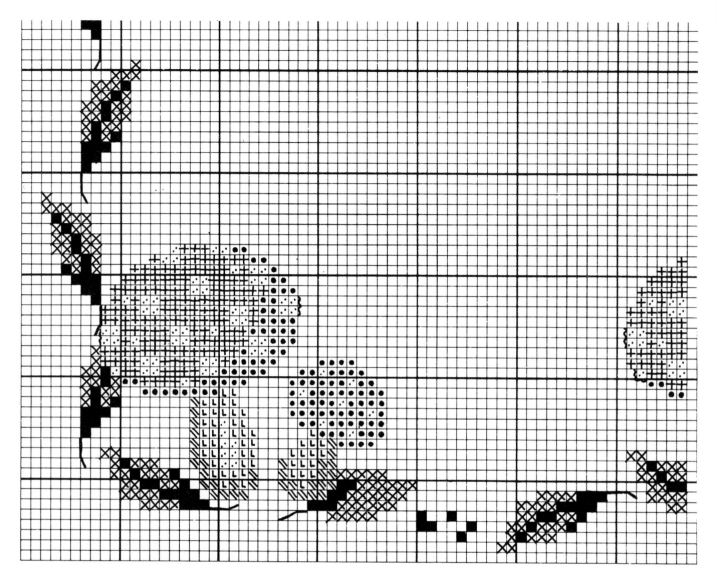

×××××××× The Bedroom

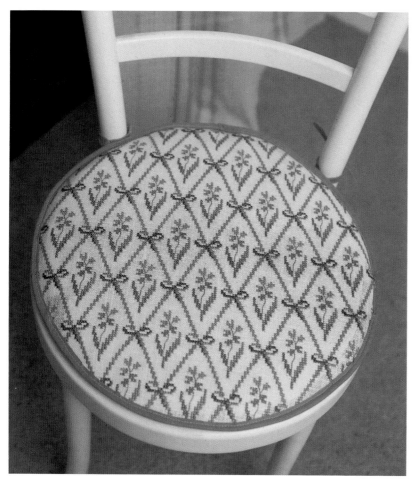

Plate 21. Chair Seat
with Flowers and Blue Bows

Plate 22. Bedroom Rug

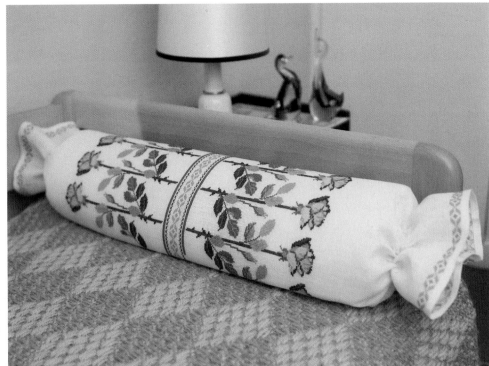

Plate 23.
Bolster Pillow
with Roses

Plate 24. Border for Dressing Table

Plate 25. Round Pincushion and Pincushion with Roses

Plate 26.
BATH Sign

Plate 27. Shelf Border with Stylized Flower

Plate 28. Bath Towels with Flowers and Hearts

Plate 29. Bathroom Nameplates

Plate 30.
Finger Towel with
Grass and Butterflies

Plate 31. Teddy Bear Pillow

Plate 32. Blind with Ducks

Plate 29. Bathroom Nameplates

Plate 30.
Finger Towel with
Grass and Butterflies

Plate 31. Teddy Bear Pillow

Plate 32. Blind with Ducks

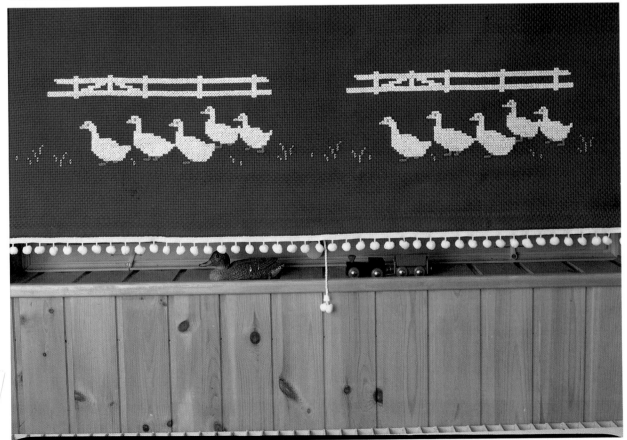

Plate 33. Children's Wastepaper Basket

Plate 34. Wallhanging
with Penguins

Plate 35. Teenager's Bulletin Board

✕✕ CHAIR SEAT WITH FLOWERS AND BLUE BOWS

See Plate 21.

Finished size and cutting size depend on size of seat (see Instructions)

Materials

Linen with 20 threads/in. (8/cm.)
DMC embroidery yarn, 2 skeins for each color, except gold (3 skeins)
Colored cotton piping or bias tape
Cotton backing the same size as the linen

Instructions

Place a sheet of paper over your chair and draw the outline of the seat, leaving 1 cm. extra for seam and shrinkage allowance. Place the pattern on the linen and baste along the outline. Find the center of the fabric and the center of one of the bows and begin from there. Use 3 strands of yarn in the needle over 2 threads of fabric. When you have finished, cut the top and back of the seat cushion according to the paper pattern. Place foam rubber or other washable padding between the two layers and stitch them together. Stitch the colored piping over the seam.

DMC *yarn*

✕	680	golden
●	469	green
+	470	light green
○	351	red
∴	352	light red
◣	312	blue
⁄⁄	334	light blue

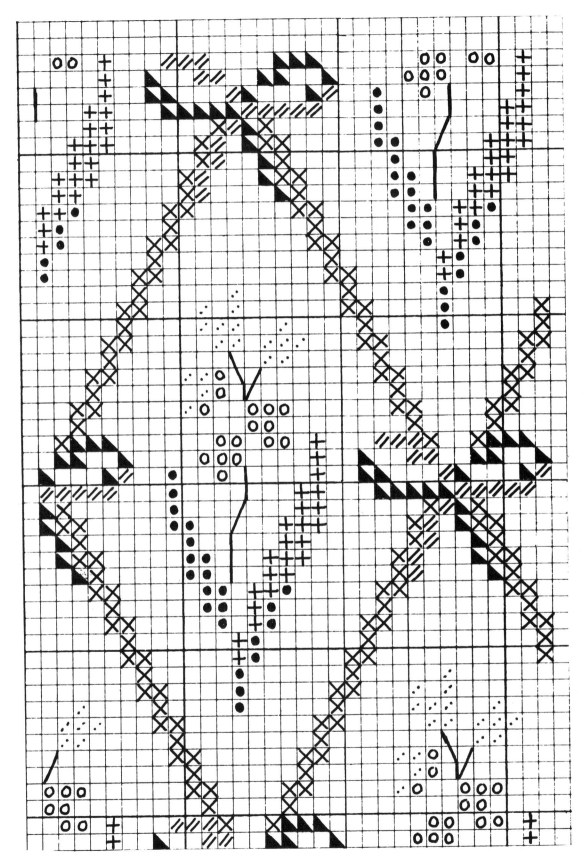

✕✕ BEDROOM RUG

See Plate 22.

Finished size and cutting size can be whatever the floor space requires. See the formula on page 11 to help estimate size.

Materials

Any coarse, soft fabric in an open or basket weave that has 5 stitches/in. 2/cm.)
Any kind of yarn can be used, as long as it covers the fabric completely
Colored fringe

Instructions

Stitch the design according to the chart. Hem the rug all the way around and sew the fringe at the two shorter edges.

Yarn

dull green
green
red

BEDROOM RUG

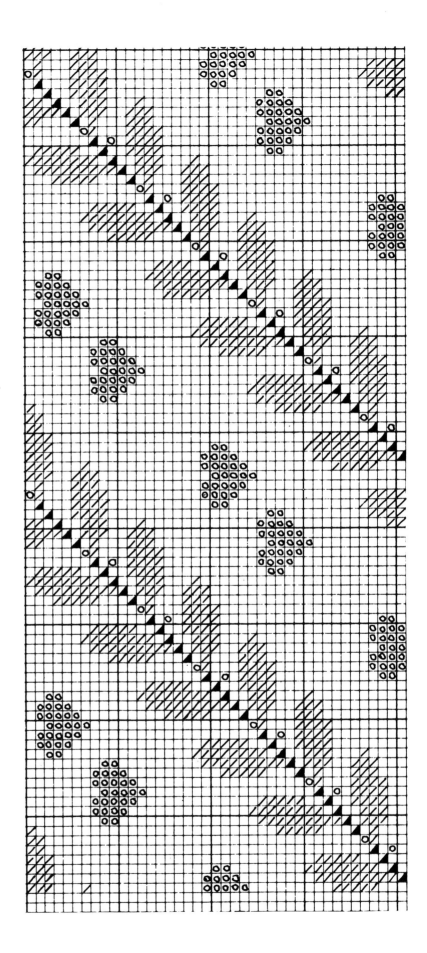

BOLSTER PILLOW WITH ROSES

See Plate 23.

Finished size: 30 × 6³/₄″ (85 × 17 cm. in diameter)
Cutting size: 36 × 24″ (90 × 60 cm.)

Materials

Linen with 25 threads/in. (10/cm.)
DMC embroidery yarn, about 3 or 4 skeins per color
Pillow 24″ (60 cm.) long and 6³/₄″ (17 cm.) in diameter

Instructions

Find the center of the fabric and begin by stitching the center band. Use 2 strands of yarn in the needle over 2 threads. The borders on the two ends of the pillow are simply the inside design from this band. When finished, place the two long sides right sides facing, and sew them together. Turn the case right side out, put the pillow inside, and tie the ends with string or colored yarn.

DMC yarn

◣	3345	darkest green, 2 skeins
⫽	3346	dark green, 2 skeins
⊠	3347	medium green, 2 skeins
|	471	light green, 2 skeins
✕	731	dull green, 1 skein
●	315	dark dull lilac, 2 skeins
■	349	bright red, 1 skein
◥	892	dark rose, 1 skein
○	740	orange, 1 skein
⌐	972	yellow, 1 skein
∴	444	light yellow, 1 skein

BOLSTER PILLOW WITH ROSES

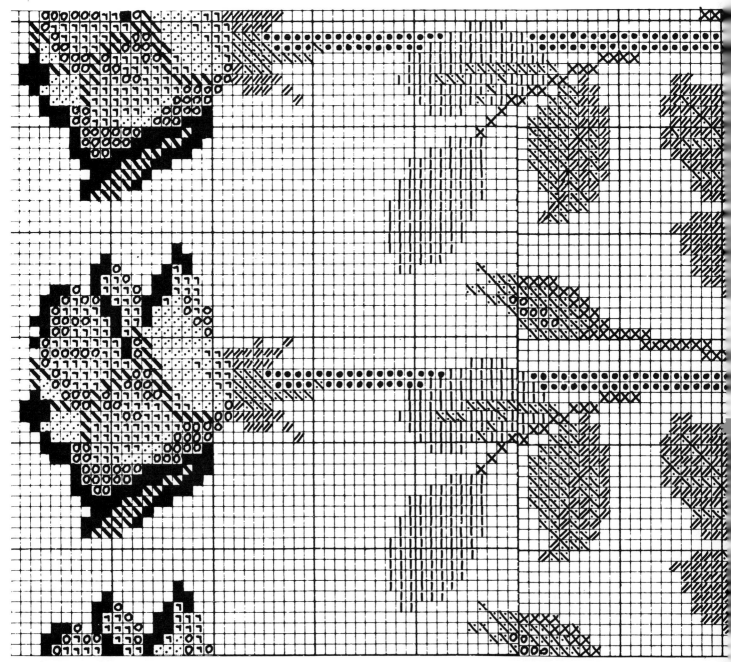

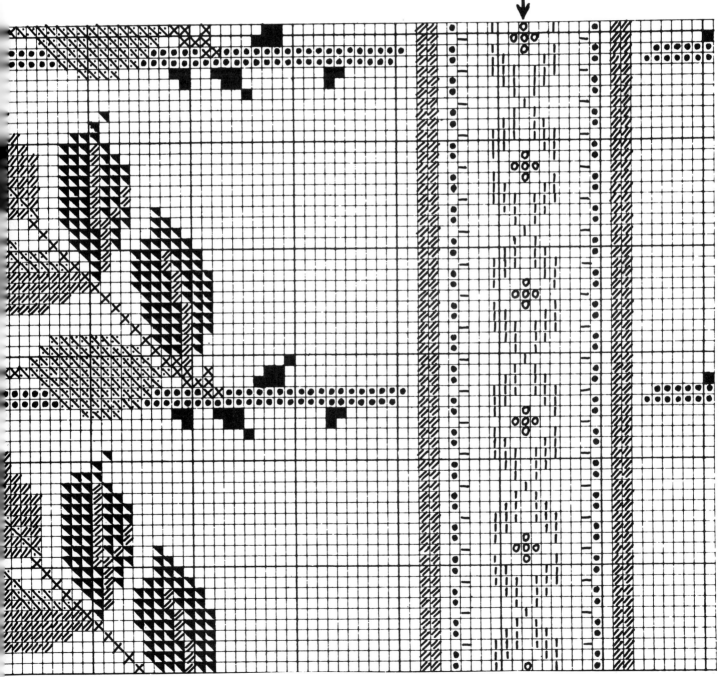

✕✕ BORDER FOR DRESSING TABLE

See Plate 24.

Finished size: 1⅝″ (4 cm.) deep and as long as your table
Cutting size: 4″ (10 cm.) deep and as long as your table, plus 1½″ (3 cm.) for hem

Materials

Linen with 25 threads/in. (10/cm.)
DMC embroidery yarn, one skein of each color
One piece of medium-weight interfacing, such as Pellon® nonwoven bonded textiles, the same size as the finished embroidery

Instructions

Embroider the motif according to the diagram, using 2 strands of yarn in the needle over 2 threads of fabric. Place the finished embroidery face down and center the interfacing on it. Turn back the edges of the linen over the interfacing and sew it to the back with small stitches. Fasten to your dressing table with strong glue.

DMC yarn

◣	931	dark blue-gray
✕	932	light blue-gray
●	3012	faded green
L	471	light green
╱	108	orange

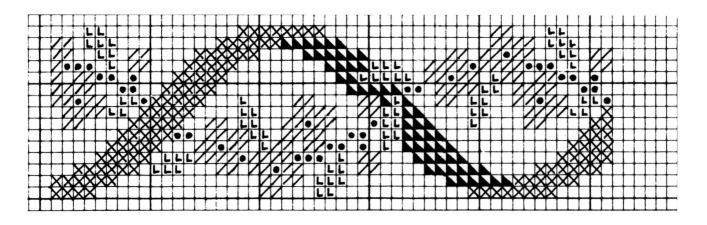

✕✕ ROUND PINCUSHION

See Plate 25.

Finished size: 4¹/₂″ (11 cm. in diameter)
Cutting size: 5″ (13 cm.) in diameter (cut two pieces, one for the front,
    one for the back)

Materials

Linen with 20 threads/in. (8/cm.)
DMC embroidery yarn, one skein for each color
Cotton wool stuffing

Instructions

Embroider the motif according to the diagram, using 3 strands of yarn in the needle. Sew the front and back sections together, inside out (right sides together), leaving 2¹/₂ inches (6 cm.) open for stuffing. Turn right side out, fill with cotton wool, and carefully stitch closed.

DMC yarn

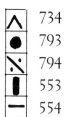

⋏	734	golden
●	793	blue
⦙	794	light blue
❙	553	lilac
—	554	light lilac

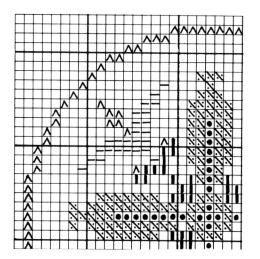

PINCUSHION WITH ROSES

See Plate 25.

Finished size: 6 × 4″ (14.5 × 9.5 cm.)
Cutting size: 7 × 5″ (18 × 13 cm.)

Materials

Linen with 20 threads/in. (8/cm.)
DMC embroidery yarn, one skein for each color
Cotton wool stuffing

Instructions

Find the center of the fabric and the design (marked with a cross). Use this to start your counting. Use 3 strands of yarn in the needle over 2 threads of fabric. When the embroidery is done, complete the pincushion according to instructions for the preceding project, the round pincushion.

DMC yarn

469	dark green
470	medium green
3348	light green
309	dark rose
899	medium rose
776	light rose
733	faded green

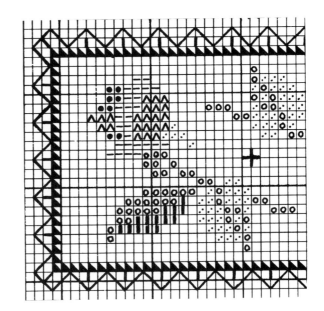

74

XXXXXXXXX # The Bathroom

✕✕ BATH SIGN

See Plate 26.

Finished size: 6³/₄ × 4¹/₂″ (17 × 11 cm.)
Cutting size: 9 × 5¹/₂″ (22 × 14 cm.)
Cardboard (white): 6³/₄ × 4¹/₂″ (17 × 11 cm.)

Materials

Linen with 20 threads/in. (8/cm.)
DMC embroidery yarn, one skein of each color

Instructions

Find the center of the fabric and of the design and count your stitches from there, using 3 strands of yarn in the needle. Press the finished embroidery. With the embroidered side face down, lay the cardboard in the center of the wrong side and turn the edges of the linen under. Glue them to the cardboard.

DMC yarn

◣	300	brown
●	900	red
╱	905	dark green
∧	906	medium green
—	907	light green
■	731	dull green

BATH SIGN

SHELF BORDER WITH STYLIZED FLOWER

See Plate 27.

Finished size: 2³/₄″ (4.5 cm.) deep and as long as your shelf
Cutting size: 4¹/₂″ (11 cm.) deep and as long as your shelf, plus 1¹/₂ inches
    (3 cm.) to hem

Materials

Linen with 25 threads/in. (10/cm.)
DMC embroidery yarn, one skein of each color
One piece of medium-weight interfacing, such as Pellon® nonwoven
    bonded textiles, the same size as the finished embroidery

Instructions

Stitch the motif according to the graph, using 2 strands of yarn in the needle. Press the finished embroidery. Place the interfacing on top of the wrong side, turn the edges of the linen to the back, and sew together with small stitches. This will help keep the shelf border stiff. Glue it to the edge of your cosmetics shelf to liven up your bathroom cabinet.

DMC yarn

■	830	brown
◥	335	dark rose
L	894	light rose
●	906	green

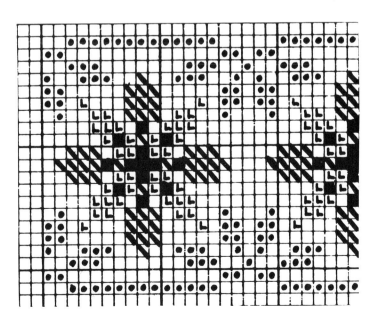

✕✕ BATH TOWELS WITH FLOWERS AND HEARTS

See Plate 28.

Finished size: 1¼″ (3 cm.) and as long as your towel is wide
Cutting size: 1½″ (4 cm.) and as long as your towel is wide

Materials

Cotton, with about 15 threads/in. (6/cm.)
DMC embroidery yarn, one skein of each color
Terry-cloth towels

Instructions

Stitch the designs according to the graphs, using 2 threads of yarn in the needle. Iron the finished embroidery and fold over the long sides to make a small hem. Stitch the border to your towel using small backstitches (for the floral border), or machine stitch it on (for the heart border) in the color of your towel.

DMC yarn

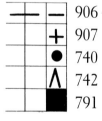

—	906	green
+	907	light green
●	740	dark orange
∧	742	light orange
■	791	dark blue

DMC yarn

X	899	red
●		gold metal

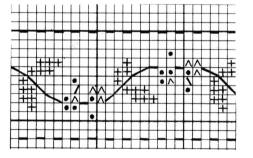

80

✕✕ BATHROOM NAMEPLATES

See Plate 29.

Finished size: 3³/₄ × 1⁵/₈″ (9.25 × 4 cm.)
Cutting size: 5 × 2¹/₂″ (12 × 6 cm.)
Cardboard (white): 3³/₄ × 1⁵/₈″ (9.25 × 4 cm.)

Materials

Linen with 30 threads/in. (12/cm.)
DMC embroidery yarn, one skein of each color

Instructions

Find the center of the fabric and of the design and count your stitches from there, using one strand of yarn in the needle. Place the cardboard on top of the wrong side, turn up the edges of the linen to the back, and fasten with small stitches or glue. Attach the nameplates to your bathroom tiles or wall with strong adhesive.

DMC *yarn*

◣	937	dark green
⁄⁄	470	light green
—	315	red-brown
●	798	dark blue
+	793	light blue
C	210	light lilac
∴		white

BATHROOM NAMEPLATES

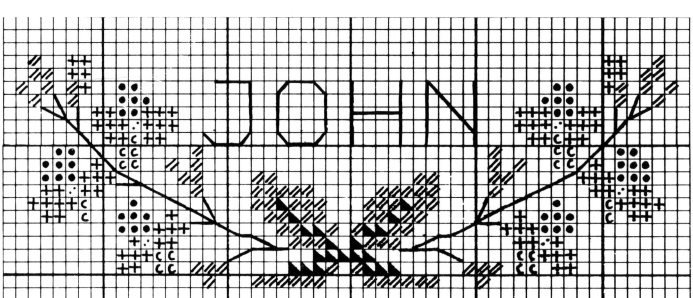

✕✕ FINGER TOWEL WITH GRASS AND BUTTERFLIES

See Plate 30.

Finished size: 12½ × 21″ (31 × 52 cm.)
Cutting size: 14 × 21″ (35 × 52 cm.)

Materials

Beige aida (imitation gauze) with 12 threads/in. (5/cm.)
DMC embroidery yarn, one skein of each color

Instructions

Begin embroidering the borders 1 inch (2.5 cm.) from the edges, making a ¼ inch (1 cm.) wide hem. Use 3 strands of yarn in the needle. Leave a 1 inch (2.5 cm.) fray at both ends. Find the center between the borders and begin embroidering the grass, counting from the arrow.

DMC yarn

—	●	223	dull red
	◣	580	dark green
	✕	3053	light green
	■	610	brown
	∟	793	blue
	•⁺	809	light blue

FINGER TOWEL WITH
GRASS AND BUTTERFLIES

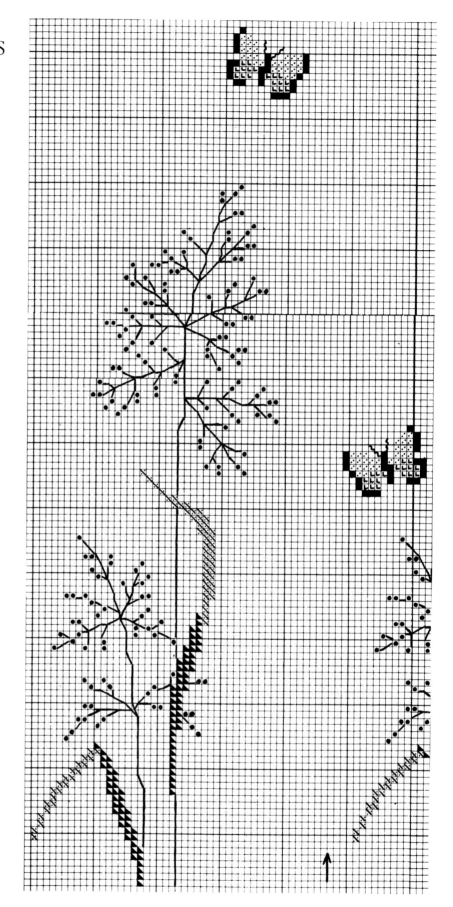

XXXXX **The Children's Room**

✕✕ TEDDY BEAR PILLOW

See Plate 31.

Finished size: 17 × 17″ (42 × 42 cm.)
Cutting size: 18 × 18″ (45 × 45 cm.)

Materials

Green burlap with 15 threads/in. (6/cm.)
About 2 yards (2 m.) cord in a suitable color
DMC embroidery yarn, 4 skeins of gold, 2 skeins of white, 1 skein of dark
    brown, 1 skein of brown, 1 skein each of light and dark lilac

Instructions

Find the center of the design and of the material. Begin cross-stitching from there, using 4 strands of yarn in the needle to cover 2 threads of fabric per stitch. Iron the finished design and cut a piece of burlap for the back the same size as the front. Place both sides together, right sides facing, and stitch, leaving the bottom side open for the zipper. Sew zipper into the fourth side. Stitch cord around seam on all four sides. Fill with pillow the appropriate size.

DMC yarn

◣	3031	dark brown
─●	781	brown
∧	783	golden
•∴	739	light golden
◼	552	dark lilac
I	554	light lilac

TEDDY BEAR PILLOW

✕✕ BLIND WITH DUCKS

See Plate 32.

Finished size: 40 × 60″ (100 × 150 cm.)
Cutting size: 43 × 67″ (110 × 170 cm.)

Materials

Blue cotton imitation gauze with 24 stitches per 4 in. (10 cm.)
DMC Matania yarn
Pom-pom fringe

Instructions

Begin embroidering midway across the material and about 8 inches (20 cm.) from bottom, starting with the midpoint of the design. Use 1 strand of cotton yarn in the needle, covering 1 thread of fabric per stitch. Iron the finished piece and hem the long sides, making a casing about 1 inch (2.5 cm.) at the bottom for the bar. Iron the piece and glue the top of the material to the "rolling bar." Sew on the pom-pom border.

DMC yarn

white
2740 orange
2726 yellow
2434 light brown
2907 green

BLIND WITH DUCKS

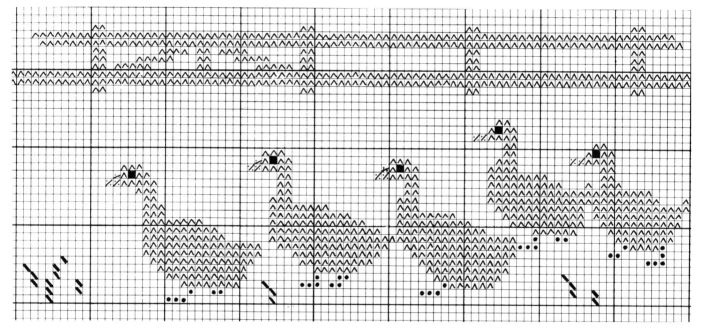

✕✕ CHILDREN'S WASTEPAPER BASKET

See Plate 33.

Finished size: 11 × 29″ (28 × 73 cm.)
Cutting size: 18 × 30½″ (45 × 76 cm.)
(These measurements may vary, depending on the size of your wastepaper
    basket)

Materials

Burlap with 15 threads/in. (6/cm.)
DMC embroidery yarn, 3 or 4 skeins of each color
One round tub or wastepaper basket

Instructions

Cut your material according to the size of your wastebasket. Count 1½ inches (3 cm.) for
a hem at the bottom and about 5½ inches (14 cm.) to be folded over the top, inside the
tub. Stitch the design about 1½ inches (3 cm.) from the bottom edge, using 4 strands of
yarn in the needle over 2 threads of fabric. Iron the finished piece and glue the burlap to
the tub.

DMC yarn

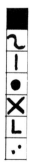

■	830	brown
∿	444	yellow
I	445	light yellow
●	906	green
✕	907	light green
L	827	light blue
∴		white

CHILDREN'S WASTEPAPER BASKET

✕✕ WALLHANGING WITH PENGUINS

See Plate 34.

Finished size: 16½ × 20½″ (41 × 51 cm.)
Cutting size: 18 × 24″ (45 × 60 cm.)

Materials

Blue hessian burlap, 15 threads/in. (6/cm.)
DMC embroidery yarn, 6 skeins of black, 6 of white, and one each of dark
    and light gray
Bamboo or brass rods, 2 pieces, 20½″ (51 cm.) long

Instructions

Find the center of the fabric and of the design (use the arrows) and count your stitches from there. Use 4 strands of yarn in the needle and cover 2 threads of fabric per stitch. Count 6 cm. from the motif to the edges and hem the long sides. Count 10 cm. to the top and the bottom and make a 2.5 cm. casing to insert bamboo fittings.

    For hemming and finishing instructions see page 23.

DMC yarn

●	310	black
∧	645	dark gray
I	648	light gray
∴		white
～	921	rust

WALLHANGING WITH PENGUINS

✕✕ TEENAGER'S BULLETIN BOARD

See Plate 35.

Finished size: 39½ × 23" (99 × 58 cm.)
Cutting size: 44 × 28" (110 × 70 cm.)

Materials

Colored burlap, 15 threads/in. (6/cm.)
DMC white pearl cotton #5, 6 skeins per in. (2.5/cm.)
Styrofoam or corkboard, 39½ × 23" (99 × 58 cm.)

Instructions

Begin embroidery 4½ inches (11 cm.) from the edge of the fabric. Cross stitches are made with one strand of yarn in the needle over 2 threads of fabric. Iron the finished embroidery, and center the Styrofoam or corkboard behind it. Fold over the extra material and fasten it to the board with pins or staples.